Remembering
Norfolk

Peggy Haile McPhillips

TURNER
PUBLISHING COMPANY

How many modes of transportation can be spotted in this view of a busy Granby Street at City Hall Avenue on a summer day in 1913? Horses and buggies vie with automobiles, streetcars, pedestrians, and probably a bicycle or two just out of view.

Remembering Norfolk

Turner Publishing Company
4507 Charlotte Avenue • Suite 100
Nashville, Tennessee 37209
(615) 255-2665

Remembering Norfolk

www.turnerpublishing.com

Library of Congress Control Number: 2010926210

ISBN: 9781596526860

Printed in the United States of America

ISBN: 978-1-68336-861-8 (pbk)

CONTENTS

Ocean View Park in 1920, with the Ocean View Hotel in the foreground. There are at least as many people strolling the boardwalk or relaxing on benches in the park as there are in the water.

ACKNOWLEDGMENTS

This volume, *Remembering Norfolk,* is the result of the cooperation and efforts of many individuals and organizations. It is with great thanks that we acknowledge the valuable contribution of the following for their generous support:

The Sargeant Memorial Room, Norfolk Public Library
The Harry C. Mann Collection of the Library of Virginia
Library of Congress

We would also like to thank the following individuals for valuable contributions and assistance in making this work possible:

W. Troy Valos, for his discovery of many unprinted negatives in the Norfolk Public Library collection; Terry McPhillips, for giving up use of the dining room table and many weekends while his wife was laying out this book; and all the gentlemen on the other side of the lens—photographers such as Harry C. Mann, Charles Borjes, H. D. Vollmer, Carroll Walker, and more, who captured our triumphs, our tragedies, and glimpses into our everyday lives, represented on the pages of this book.

PREFACE

Norfolk has thousands of historic photographs that reside in archives, both locally and nationally. This book began with the observation that, while those photographs are of great interest to many, they are not easily accessible. During a time when Norfolk is looking ahead and evaluating its future course, many people are asking, How do we treat the past? These decisions affect every aspect of the state—architecture, public spaces, commerce, infrastructure—and these, in turn, affect the way that people live their lives. This book seeks to provide easy access to a valuable, objective look into the history of Norfolk.

Although the photographer can make subjective decisions regarding subject matter and how to capture and present it, photographs, unlike words, seldom interpret history subjectively. This lends them an authority that textual histories sometimes fail to achieve, and offers the viewer an original, untainted perspective from which to draw his own conclusions, interpretations, and insights.

This project represents countless hours of review and research. The writer has reviewed thousands of photographs in numerous archives and greatly appreciates the generous assistance of the archivists listed in the acknowledgments of this work, without whom this project could not have been completed.

The goal in publishing this work is to provide broader access to this set of extraordinary photographs that seek to inspire, provide perspective, and evoke insight that might assist people who are responsible for determining Norfolk's future. In addition, the book seeks to preserve the past with adequate respect and reverence.

With the exception of touching up imperfections that have accrued with the passage of time and cropping where necessary, no changes have been made. The focus and clarity of many images are limited to the technology and the ability of the photographer at the time they were recorded.

The work is divided into eras. Beginning with some of the earliest known photographs of Norfolk, the first section records photographs through the first five years of the twentieth century. The second section continues with the early years of the twentieth century through World War I and up to 1920. Section Three moves from the 1920s through World War II. The last section covers the postwar era to the early 1960s. In each of these sections we have made an effort to capture various aspects of life through our selection of photographs. People, commerce, transportation, infrastructure, religious institutions, and educational institutions have been included to provide a broad perspective.

We encourage readers to reflect as they go walking in Norfolk, strolling through the city, its parks, and its neighborhoods. It is the publisher's hope that in utilizing this work, longtime residents will learn something new and that new residents will gain a perspective on where Norfolk has been, so that each can contribute to its future.

—*Todd Bottorff, Publisher*

The Stone Bridge, also known as the Humpback Bridge, was built in 1818 to connect south Granby Street with north Granby Street, spanning Town Back Creek. The improved access enabled the development of a residential community to the north of the original town. Town Back Creek was completely filled by 1905 and is the site of City Hall Avenue today.

War and Peace and a New Century

(1860s–1905)

The side-wheel steamer USS *Fort Donelson* was built in Scotland in 1860 as the *Giraffe*. She served briefly as the Confederate blockade runner *Robert E. Lee* before being captured in November 1863 and converted into a warship for the Union Navy, assigned to the North Atlantic Blockading Squadron. She assisted in the capture of Fort Fisher and is seen here at the Norfolk Navy Yard in December 1864.

The first carload of coal arrived in Norfolk by rail from West Virginia in 1883 and soon replaced cotton as Norfolk's number one export. Coal and cargo piers were moved from downtown to this location, Lamberts Point, in 1886, and a residential community soon developed to house and serve the workers and their families. By 1900, Norfolk was the leading coal-exporting port on the East Coast—the industry continued to grow even through the Great Depression. Lamberts Point was annexed to the city of Norfolk in 1911.

The Norfolk Academy, around 1892. Norfolk Academy was founded in 1804. Thomas U. Walter of Philadelphia, Architect of the United States Capitol, designed this building for the private boys' academy in 1840, patterning it after the Grecian-Doric Temple of Theseus at Athens. It served as a hospital for Union soldiers during the Civil War and as the Norfolk post office during the yellow fever epidemic of 1855. The Academy occupied the building until 1916. Today it serves as the headquarters for the Hampton Roads Chamber of Commerce.

Main Street at Commercial Place, seen here around 1900, was the site of Norfolk's earliest commercial district. When Norfolk County Surveyor John Ferebee laid out the original Norfolk Town on his 1680 survey, he designated this site for a marketplace, and it continued to serve this role for more than 200 years. Although the horse-drawn drays filled with product from Princess Anne and Norfolk counties are gone, the commercial aspect remains. Today, lined with towering banks and office buildings, the site is the location of Norfolk's financial district.

Built at the northwest corner of Granby Street and College Place in 1880 as the College for Young Ladies, this building became the Algonquin Hotel around 1900. Later renamed the Lee, the structure burned in 1983 and the site is occupied today by the Tidewater Community College.

Members of the First Baptist Church congregation on Bute Street, around 1880. The Baptist Church was established in Norfolk in 1800 and was formally organized in 1805, with an interracial congregation. The white members separated in 1815 to form a new congregation. The remaining African-American congregation took the name First Baptist Church Bute Street at that time. The congregation worshiped in the building pictured here from 1877 to 1904.

Election Day in 1903 was a boisterous affair, as voters turned out to elect candidates to the Virginia House of Delegates. Anticipating trouble at the polls, Police Chief M. J. Vellines posted officers at each precinct to break up crowds and fights. As a result, only three fights were reported, one at the first precinct of the first ward, a vacant store at the northeast corner of Main and Fenchurch streets, shown here at a calmer moment.

Seen here in 1904, the Hospital of St. Vincent DePaul was established in 1856 in the former home of Ann Plume Behan Herron, who had opened her Church Street home to victims of yellow fever the previous year. Miss Herron died of the fever, but her legacy survives. She left her home and estate to the Daughters of Charity so that they might establish Norfolk's first public hospital. St. Vincent's was housed here until moving to its current location on Granby Street in 1944. It was transferred to the Bon Secours Health System in 1996.

The street trolley chugs west along Main Street, about to turn north onto Granby around the turn of the century. On the near left is the Stevens Furniture Building, constructed in 1869 after the design of Baltimore architect Edmund Lind. Many Norfolk citizens set their watches by the large clock outside Citizens' Bank Building, on the right.

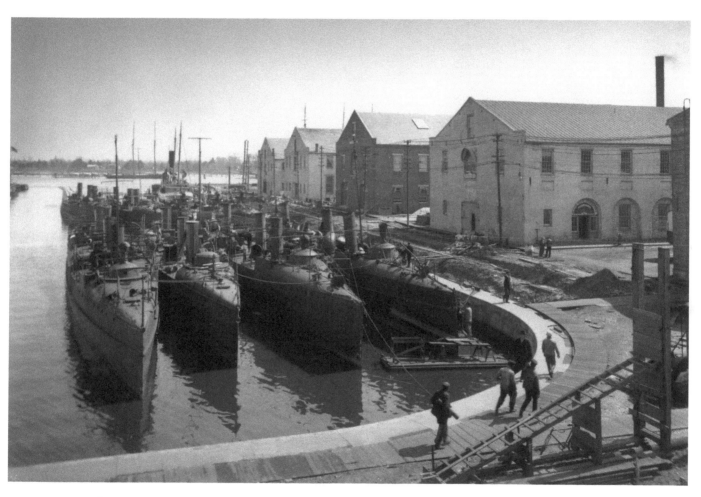

In the Norfolk Navy Yard in 1905, torpedo boats probably assigned to the Reserve Torpedo Flotilla wait in wet dock.

The Ocean View Hotel, around 1905. With its wraparound wooden porch, the hotel offered guests a respite from the summer sun, while music from the bandstand, at left provided an evening's accompaniment to the gentle sounds of the surf and children being called in from play. An amusement ride appears to be in motion at right.

The World at Our Door

(1906–1920)

The Union Mission on Church Street, early 1900s. The Norfolk Union Mission was founded in 1892 to serve homeless and impoverished men. The Mission occupied this building on Church Street until moving to East Main Street in 1919. Amenities including beds, meals, showers, and a reading room were provided to residents, as well as nightly and Sunday nondenominational religious services. One of the gentlemen on the sidewalk demonstrates another amenity: free ice water.

The 1907 Jamestown Exposition at Sewells Point in Norfolk County was both entertaining and educational. This relief map of the Panama Canal, then under construction, was created by the Isthmian Canal Commission. The map was 122 feet by 60 feet, with its concrete surface roughened and painted green to represent land. Scale models of ships tow to five inches long "sailed" along the Canal's course, demonstrating the size of the largest ships then in operation and the largest projected.

The Jamestown Exposition Auditorium sits at the center of this scene, with the Palaces of Education occupying its east and west wings. The Fine Art Building lies to the right of the Auditorium, and the Marine Exhibits Building to the left.

Twenty-sixth United States President Theodore Roosevelt was a guest at the Jamestown Exposition two times—on opening day, shown here, and on Georgia Day, which honored his mother's native state. He returned on December 16, 1907, to participate in the send-off of the Great White Fleet on a round-the-world cruise meant to demonstrate American naval power.

The Norfolk & Portsmouth Traction company built this passenger station, seen here around 1908, at its Ocean View terminus shortly after the turn of the century. The station was particularly busy during the summer months, as vacationers poured from the cars with their trunks and suitcases for lengthy stays in the guest cottages that lined the beach, while locals debarked for day excursions at Ocean View Park or picnics overlooking the Chesapeake Bay.

The Marine Bank was organized in July 1872 and for many years occupied its own building, shown here, at the northwest corner of Main and Bank streets. The Marine Bank's assets and liabilities were taken over by the National Bank of Commerce in 1921. Behind the bank, on Bank Street, Steve Seelinger's cafe and buffet was a popular place to lunch.

The introduction of rail service to Ocean View by the Norfolk Traction Company in 1879 greatly accelerated the growth of the community. The Traction Company set up the first rides at its Ocean View terminus in 1899; by the turn of the century, the area was a popular summer resort. The traditional cowcatcher on the front of the car, seen here around 1908, may never have caught a cow in Norfolk, but it was a popular challenge for youngsters to catch a ride on it until the conductor chased them away.

A photographer recorded Norfolk's buisness community in the vicinity of East Main and Water streets in 1919. The Tagliavia Grocery and Fruit Market, operated by Anthony and Philip Tagliavia, stood at 908 ½ East Main Street.

A paid fire department was established by Norfolk City Council in 1871 to replace a series of volunteer companies that too often lacked the training or equipment to do a proper job of fighting fires in the growing city. A headquarters building was completed in 1872, and outlying stations were added as Norfolk continued to grow by annexation. The Berkley station, shown here in 1915, was completed shortly after the town of Berkley was annexed to the city of Norfolk in 1906.

A barefoot, middy-bloused youngster appears to be supervising his elders as they prepare to pave Church Street along the newly laid streetcar tracks in front of the Atlantic Auction House and N. S. Horton Grocers, around 1910.

The Pickwick Club and Billiard Parlors opened in the former Y.M.C.A. building on Main Street around 1912. Amenities on the upper floors were supplemented by those at street level—Henderson's Restaurant and Harry Tabb's Bar, both of which were open to the public as well as to Pickwick members.

The interior of the Pickwick Billiard Parlors, where players might choose straight-rail or pocket billiards, and where there was plenty of seating for spectators.

Main Street at Commercial Place, January 3, 1918. A mule-drawn sleigh makes its way through the snow around the base of the Confederate Monument at Commercial Place. During this coldest winter on record in Norfolk, the Elizabeth River froze solid and the adventurous crossed the river between Norfolk and Portsmouth by sleigh or on foot. Could the passenger in the sleigh have been a Portsmouth resident come to observe the detritus from the New Year's Day 1918 fire?

The Naval Y.M.C.A. was established in rented quarters in a three-story building on Church Street in 1902. This stunning building on Brooke Avenue opened in February 1909, with a formal dedication on March 17, 1909. The Navy Y was a gift from John D. Rockefeller to the enlisted men of the Navy.

An elaborate arch festooned with bunting greeted President William Howard Taft on his visit to Norfolk on November 19, 1909. Taft made several trips to Norfolk during his presidency, usually staying in a private room over Seelinger's Restaurant on Bank Street and making day trips to Princess Anne County to hunt game.

At the Chesapeake and Ohio rail station on Brooke Avenue, President Taft waits in his car for the parade in his honor to begin. The president was a large man, famous for his appetite. On this visit, it was reported that he downed between a few dozen and three barrels of oysters at one sitting. The number grew with the retelling of the tale.

Pedestrians intermingle with electric streetcars and horse-drawn wagons and buggies in this busy Main Street vista looking east from Commerce. The Saks store to the left sold men's clothing and furnishings. The building with columns a few doors down was occupied by the Norfolk Bank for Savings and Trust.

The two-horse-powered Engine Number Five races down East Main Street on the morning of January 4, 1918, possibly to the scene of the fire still smoldering at the Monticello Hotel from New Year's Day.

Peter Wright became Norfolk's first automobile owner in June 1900. By 1910, around the time of this photo, there were more than a dozen Norfolk companies in the business of selling, storing, repairing, or accessorizing the family motor car. Edward J. Allen's Rambler Garage & Supply Company on Granby Street specialized in repairs and supplies for Rambler and Maxwell motor cars.

A display of Tip Top Milk fills the display window at Benjamin F. Morgan & Company grocers on Main Street, possibly to remind the thoughtful shopper of the family kitty waiting at home.

St. Joseph's Catholic Church on East Queen Street (now Brambleton Avenue) around 1910. St. Joseph's Parish for African-Americans was established in Norfolk in 1889. A school and parish building were dedicated in 1893. The parish was absorbed by St. Mary's Parish in 1961.

Sometimes our transportation needs transportation. Here, a sick horse is brought by horse-drawn ambulance to Dr. Herbert Nash Holmes's Veterinary Hospital at the corner of Granby and 10th streets, around 1910. Dr. Holmes advertised his specialties as "Horses, Dogs and Cattle."

Baltimore architects James Wyatt and William Nolting designed this structure for Virginia Bank & Trust Company in 1908, employing both Greek and Roman motifs. The building housed a series of banking operations until the 1970s, and later housed the collection of Auslew Galleries. The Virginia Club, founded in 1873, moved into the building in 1997 and continues to occupy it.

The youngster at far-right in this group of Western Union messengers is Hodges Gallop, who had been working for Western Union for one month when Lewis Hine took this photo in June 1911.

Enjoying a shave and a haircut in the Atlantic Hotel barbershop on Granby Street around 1910. This was the second of three Atlantic Hotels that stood in the same location on Granby. The first two, designed by Baltimore architect Edmund Lind in 1859 and 1867, were both destroyed by fire.

The Benjamin Altschul Department Store Building on Church Street, seen here on the inside around 1910, was designed by the Norfolk architectural firm of Clarence A. Neff and Thomas P. Thompson.

The circus is in town, around 1915. A parade of circus attractions matches the pace of the electric trolley as a crowd gathers along the 300 block of Church Street to catch a preview of what awaits them under the big top.

Horses pulling drays at Commercial Place pause for a drink from their own water fountain, around 1910. As in many southern cities of the time, the designated parking space for automobiles is in a row right down the middle of the street.

Employees of the S. S. Kresge 5&10¢ Store on East Main Street prepare to set off for their annual outing in the summer of 1917.

Fire fighters on Plume Street near the Arcade Building, 1911. Norfolk's first fire station was constructed two blocks from here in 1872. The last horse-drawn equipment was taken out of service in Norfolk in 1921.

A stately lion and whimsical cherubs greet the traveler from atop the elaborate entrance to the Atlantic Hotel on lower Granby Street around 1910. This was the third and final Atlantic Hotel built on the spot, the first two having burned in 1867 and 1902. A group of young boys, working as newsies, are on hand to provide passersby with the latest headlines.

Members of the Twin City Motorcycle Club pose for the camera at Commercial Place around 1913. Norfolk and Portsmouth, our neighbor across the Elizabeth River, were known as the "Twin Cities" for many years.

Looking east to the 100 block of East Main Street in 1917, with streetcar number 2112, on the Lamberts Point line, approaching.

President Woodrow Wilson signed a bill creating a naval base—now Naval Station Norfolk—on the old Jamestown Exposition grounds on June 15, 1917. Wilson, in trademark morning coat and top hat, later visited the base to observe construction taking shape.

Proceeds from the 10-cent German Village entry fee and the sale of baked goods, postcards, and toys handcrafted by sailors such as these were sent to the German Red Cross. After the U.S. entered the war, the German ships were seized and converted to American troopships. The internees became prisoners of war and were transferred to POW camps in Georgia.

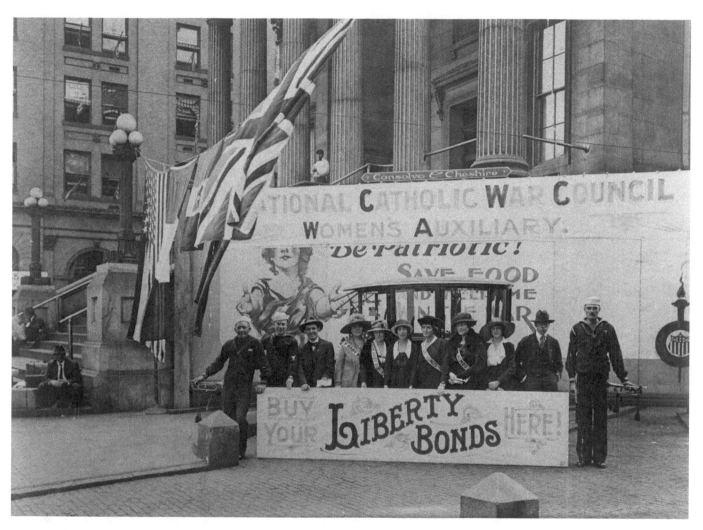

It was the Great War. While soldiers and sailors departed to fight for democracy overseas, those on the home front also did what they could to help. Here in 1918, the Norfolk unit of the National Catholic War Council Women's Auxiliary organizes a sale of Liberty Bonds at the steps of the U.S. Customhouse on Main Street, with the flags of the Allied powers hanging nearby.

The winter of 1917–18 was one of the coldest on record in Norfolk. When a fire broke out in the 200 block of Granby Street in the early morning of January 1, 1918, fire fighters rushed to the scene to fight the blaze; however, their efforts were thwarted when the water from their fire hoses froze upon contact with the frigid air, creating a scene of eerie beauty. Four nearby buildings were also destroyed and three fire fighters lost their lives. The Monticello was heavily damaged but was rebuilt the following year with two additional floors and an additional 150 guest rooms.

The Monticello Hotel around 1920, after the rebuilding. The Monticello was Norfolk's most elegant hotel for many years—its Starlight Ballroom on the top floor was the scene of many a prom and wedding reception. The building was imploded in January 1976 to make way for Norfolk's new Federal Building.

The Lorraine Hotel at Granby and Tazewell streets was one of several built to accommodate visitors to the 1907 Jamestown Exposition. Seen here around 1920, it was built on the former property of Littleton Waller Tazewell (1774–1860), one-time Virginia representative, senator, and governor. The Colonial theater, behind the Lorraine, was built around the same time. The Tazewell mansion was not demolished for the new construction, but was dismantled board by board and moved a few miles north to Edgewater, where it stands today.

Looking west on Main Street toward the river around 1920, perhaps from atop the Royster Building at Granby Street and City Hall Avenue. The Anheuser-Busch Brewing Company ceased to function as a brewery in Norfolk when Prohibition was introduced in 1920, but served as a cold storage facility for many years. A portion of the complex has been converted into condominiums and still offers a splendid view of the Elizabeth River.

Reliance Electric Company was awarded a license to operate Norfolk radio station WTAR in September 1923. It was the first radio station in Virginia. The first remote broadcasts the following year included the 1924 World Series when, for the very first time, Norfolk baseball fans were able to listen to a play-by-play account of the national pastime, as the Washington Senators defeated the New York Giants four games to three. WTAR became a CBS affiliate in 1929, a year before this station photo was taken.

A Growing City and Life on the Home Front

(1921–1945)

A fire in Berkley that began on the morning of April 14, 1922, left a wreckage trail of more than 300 homes, two churches, and 20 businesses over a ten-block area. The fire marked the end of an era for the Berkley neighborhood, as many families chose to rebuild their homes elsewhere in the growing city.

The 1922 Berkley fire began at the Tunis Lumber Company on the Berkley waterfront. Youngsters playing with matches were suspected of starting the blaze by accident, though the alleged culprits were not identified. This scene is at the Tunis docks.

More than 1,500 people were left homeless by the Berkley fire. Householders salvaged what they could as the fire approached their homes, and gathered their families and their belongings in makeshift tents. The smiling faces in this group indicate that they were more grateful for their safety than sorrowful for their losses.

Boy Scouts mass the colors as they march to a Portsmouth playground for the annual Hampton Roads Scouts' Field Day on May 26, 1923. Field Day events were followed by the dedication of Norfolk's new Boy Scout headquarters and scoutmasters' club rooms on College Place.

Market Street at Monticello Avenue, 1923.

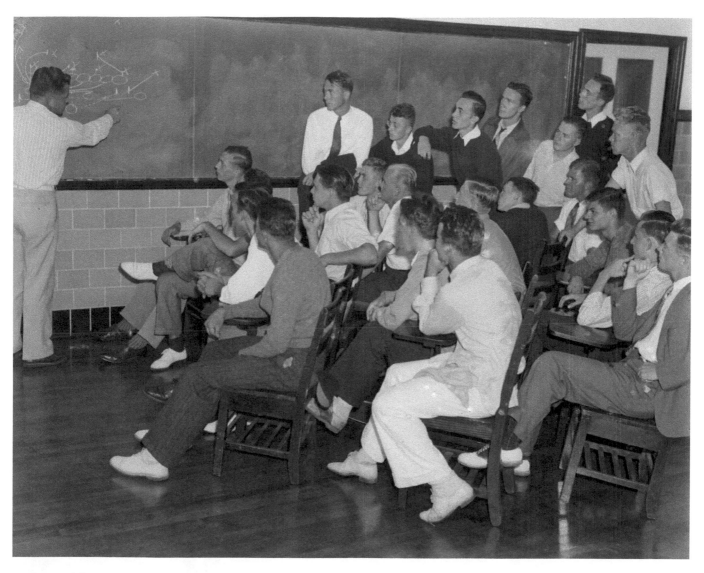

The Norfolk Division of the College of William & Mary, predecessor of today's Old Dominion University, opened in September 1930 in a two-story brick building constructed for Larchmont Elementary School in 1912. In addition to its two-year academic curriculum, the Norfolk Division established teams for football, basketball, baseball, and track, all competing as the "Braves." Thomas Lawrence "Tommy" Scott coached all four sports and taught math at the college from 1930 until he left in 1941 to join the family business. The football program ended the same year, with an overall win-lose-tie record of 62-19-4. Here, Coach Scott illustrates a play to his team.

Lon Chaney Sr. and Norma Shearer appear at the Norva Theatre in the 1924 film *He Who Gets Slapped*, while Rice's "smart woman's shop" advertises a January clearance sale in this 1926 image.

The Spartans and the Cardinals, local amateur teams playing under the auspices of the Norfolk Recreation Bureau, play an early spring game at Norfolk's Lafayette (or City) Park. The commander of the Spartans is at bat, with N. Karangelen of the Cardinals catching. The Cardinals won the game 10–7.

Former World War I pilot Ben Epstein began air taxi service between Norfolk and Richmond from his Granby Street airfield in 1929. Grand Central Air Terminal was constructed the same year and was Norfolk's first commercial airport building, promoted on this airplane in 1930.

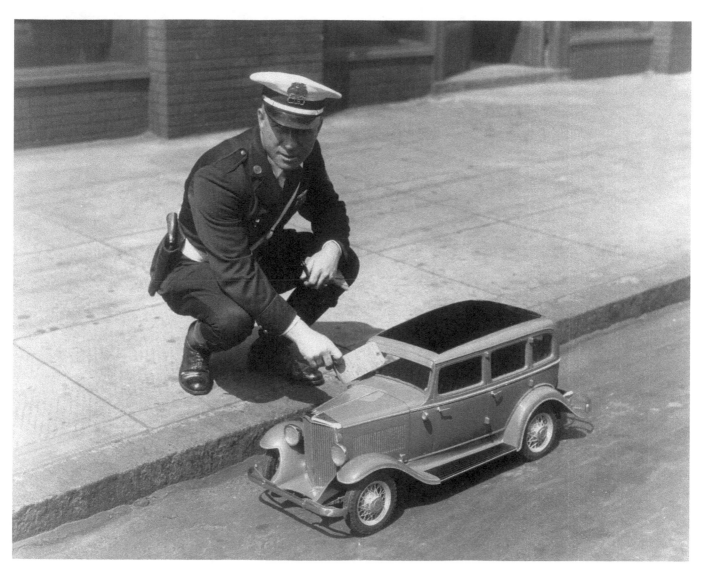

Norfolk Police Department's Officer Marshall is on the job, writing a big ticket for a tiny car, March 25, 1932.

George Herman "Babe" Ruth, the "Sultan of Swat," came to Norfolk with the New York Yankees in June 1934 for the Yankees' first exhibition game with the Norfolk Tars. Here, Ruth shakes a few hands and signs some autographs, ensuring bragging rights for these young fans in the Atlantic City neighborhood.

This airborne advertisement at the Ocean View beachfront reminds the ladies in the crowd to make a trip downtown to the Enna Jettick Store on Granby Street, where they would find just the right shoes to make them feel more "energetic."

The Norfolk Ford Plant turned out its first Model T on April 20, 1925. Norfolk mayor S. Heth Tyler, shown here, was given the honor of driving the first car off the assembly line. After more than 80 years of production, the Norfolk plant rolled out its final vehicle, a red F-150 truck, on June 28, 2007.

Passengers departing on one of the lines served by Norfolk's Union Station found a lovely place to wait for their trains inside the station, where rows of columns and an elaborate ceiling lent a sense of glamour to an otherwise ordinary journey.

The Confederate Monument towers over this Commercial Place scene. Behind the monument, the Miller, Rhoads & Swartz Department Store was a mainstay for many Norfolk shoppers well into the 1950s. Of particular interest to children was the sound of their shoes on the wooden floor in the older part of the building, and the pneumatic tubes that shot their payments out of sight then brought their change back moments later.

Not every story is a happy one. A visitor from Washington, D.C., unfamiliar with Norfolk's downtown streets and waterways, mistakenly drove his car off the end of Plume Street and into the river on a dark night in early October 1930. Sadly, he did not survive.

Bathers enjoy a day at Ocean View Beach on the Fourth of July 1931.

This wooden drawbridge served the citizens of the Campostella suburb until the area was annexed into the city of Norfolk in 1923. It was replaced by a two-lane concrete span in the latter part of 1923, but the congestion of traffic necessitated the construction in 1935 of a four-lane concrete and steel structure. The draw span from the 1923 bridge was dismantled and shipped to Pulaski County to replace the New River ferry. Today's six-lane span opened in 1987.

The hurricane-prone East Coast has seen its share of storms, but 1933 is still remembered in Norfolk as the year of the "Big One." Hurricanes in August and September 1933 brought wind speeds as high as 88 miles per hour, extensive damage at Ocean View, and 18 deaths. Here on August 23, floodwaters fill the street outside the Monticello Hotel.

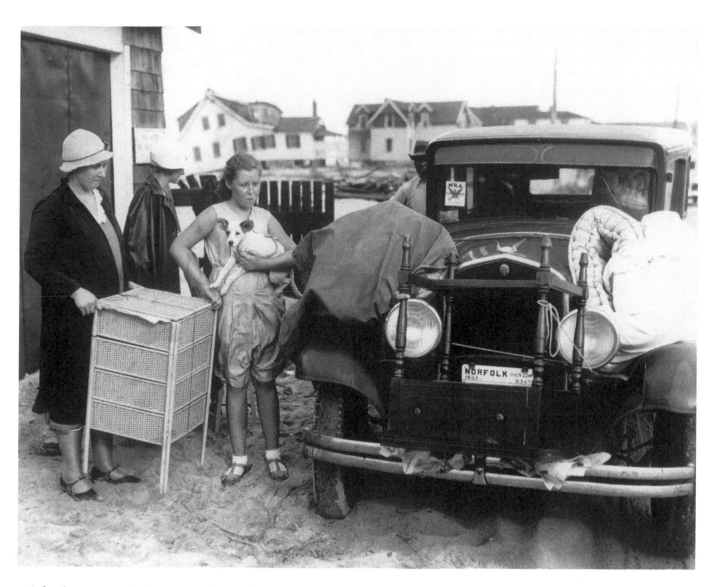

A family evacuates its Ocean View home after the hurricane, taking only what they are able to carry in—and on—the family car.

A Norfolk police officer shows off the department's brand-new emergency vehicle, used as both an ambulance and a paddy wagon, in 1933.

Boaters take advantage of the lingering high water on Granby Street after the August 1933 hurricane to put their boats in; meanwhile, their counterparts on Plume Street engaged in what they dubbed the "first annual Plume Street Regatta." After the storm passed, Norfolk took to the streets in boats and bathing suits to survey the aftereffects and be thankful that the worst was over.

Interior of the Norfolk City Market, which occupied a spot on Monticello Avenue at City Hall Avenue for more than 30 years. The motto carved above the entrance proclaimed the purpose of the market: "That pure food may be kept in the best manner and sold at a fair price."

The James Adams Floating Theater, seen here in 1932, operated in the North Carolina Sound and the Chesapeake Bay from 1914 to 1941. Edna Ferber spent a week on the boat in 1924 while gathering material and conducting research for her 1926 novel *Show Boat,* later adapted for musical theater.

The Twenty-First Street Business Men's Association used the occasion of the installation of their new street lights—said to be the brightest in the state—to throw this October 1948 street party, which they dubbed the Great White Way Jubilee. Some $40,000 in prizes—including 3 automobiles and 50 Smithfield hams—were given away, and there was free food and drink for all. The street was closed to traffic and turned into a blocks-long ballroom with several bands and a honky-tonk piano player to make feet fly. Perhaps the greatest curiosity of all amid the spectacle was the new escalator—Norfolk's first—put into operation at the Center Shops the day of the event. The escalator could convey 5,000 people an hour from the first floor to the second.

The Norfolk Division, College of William & Mary–Virginia Polytechnic Institute opened a new swimming pool in the summer of 1937 and hosted free "learn to swim" lessons to local children. The program was sponsored by the Y.M.C.A, Y.M.C.A., Norfolk School Board, and Navy Y.M.C.A. Generations of Norfolk children learned to swim in that pool.

Before there was a Greyhound or a Trailways station, bus companies such as the Carolina Coach Company, Peninsula Lines, and Norfolk Southern Bus Corporation carried passengers across the state or across the state lines from their shared depot at the City Market Building on Market Street. Their buses are shown here in 1935.

Second classmen from the United States Naval Academy load provision onto the destroyer that will take them on their summer training cruise in July 1937.

Prominent along East Main Street was the sign marking the location of Daniel "Cappy" Coleman's place of business. Coleman was a Norfolk tattoo artist famous with sailors and merchant seamen around the world and, covered with tattoos himself, was a walking advertisement for his trade. This image was taken by Farm Security Administration photographer John Vachon in March 1941. Photographers for the FSA and Office of War Administration recorded thousands of images of daily life in America during the Great Depression and World War II.

Norfolk had several short-lived air cargo and passenger terminals, beginning in 1926. In 1938, the city purchased the Truxton Golf Course east of the city limits and built the Norfolk Municipal Airport, where these officials gathered on opening day. It was the predecessor of today's Norfolk International Airport.

In this city of rivers, a network of bridges accommodates drivers, and a series of drawbridges accommodates traffic of another kind, such as the Wood Towing Company tug *Atlas,* shown passing under the Berkley Bridge in 1935.

The Norfolk Tars baseball team was formed in 1896 and played until the summer of 1955. New York Yankees owner Jacob Ruppert reorganized the Tars as a farm team of the Yankees in 1934. The Tars played at several fields during their years in Norfolk, including High Rock Park, shown here after a 1944 fire. Norfolk dentist Eddie Myers funded the rebuilding of the park, which was later renamed Myers Field in his honor.

Citizens on the home front provided many services during World War II. Some, such as the trio shown here at their station on the Government Reservation at Ocean View in September 1942, served as "spotters," watching for enemy aircraft and reporting back to the U.S. Army Air Corps.

U.S. Navy dependents have stood pierside in Norfolk to wave good-bye to their sailors for more than 300 years, but every time is much like the first—one final hug, tears wiped away, and a prayer for a safe return home.

Norfolk concrete contractor J. U. Addenbrook's Sons delivered this pile of sand to a vacant lot at the corner of Hampton Boulevard and Westover Avenue for neighbors to use in homemade bomb shelters in February 1942.

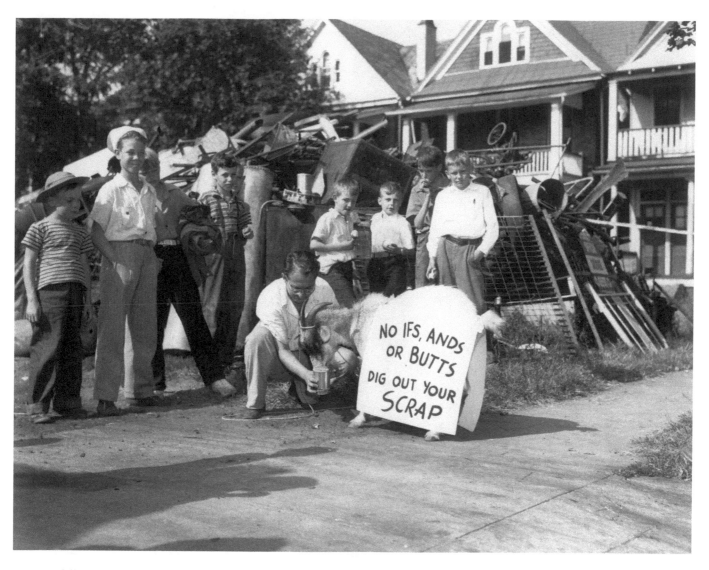

Norfolk residents of all ages—and species—worked together on the home front during World War II, collecting material such as scrap metal and rubber, as in this 1942 scrap metal drive. The material would then be converted by the government into weapons and other items for U.S. soldiers on the battlefront overseas.

Preparedness on the home front. Here, Ensign V. Taliaferro Boatwright and an assistant instruct a group of Norfolk women on the correct use of a gas mask, around 1943.

An experimental Victory garden at Lafayette Elementary School in 1943 was soon expanded into a citywide effort. Here, youngsters from Bayview Elementary School work on a victory garden behind their school in Norfolk's Ocean View section. Each of the school's 11 classes had its own plot, leading to some friendly competition and the assurance that these farmers would gladly eat their vegetables when their crops were ready to be served in the school cafeteria in June.

All in a day's work—"Big Ben" pulls a fishing boat loaded with the day's catch through the shallow surf and onto the Ocean View beach, July 14, 1944.

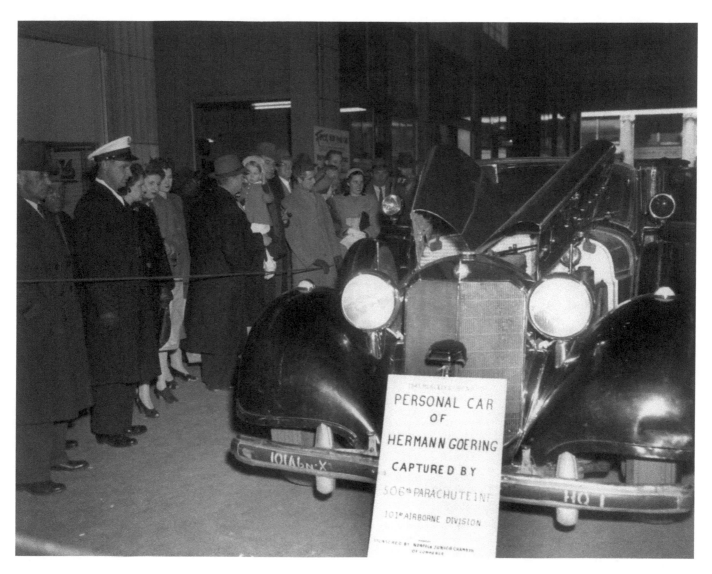

This 1943 Mercedes-Benz, said to be the personal car of Hermann Goering, is displayed in the Selden Arcade in December 1945.

There was jubilation among the Allied nations when victory over Japan was announced, heralding the end of World War II. Hearing the news, August 15, 1945, Norfolk citizens rushed downtown to take part in a frenzy of horn-blowing, street-dancing, confetti-raining euphoria.

Looking to the Future

(1946–1962)

Latvian native Elias Codd (ca. 1897–1967) arrived in Norfolk in 1910 at the age of 13 and joined the grocery trade. His sales of stamps and war bonds from his delicatessen on Princess Anne Road during World War II exceeded three million dollars. Behind his counter here in 1948, Codd continued to sell bonds into the 1960s.

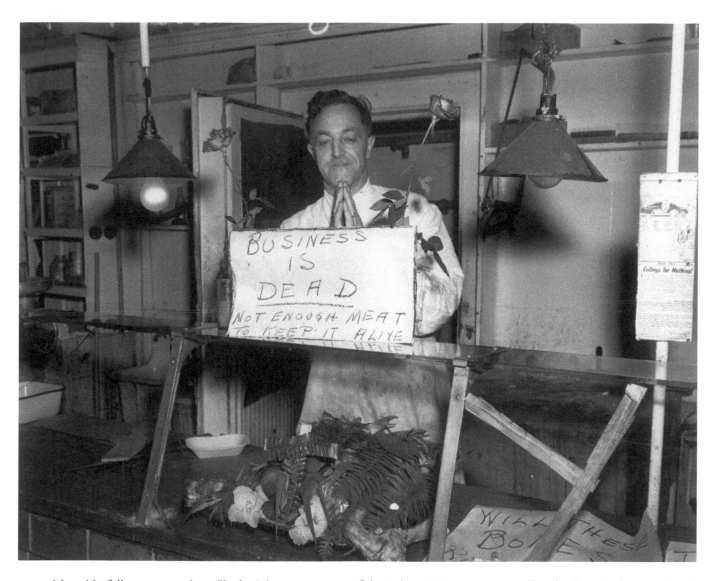

Many Norfolk grocers, such as Charles Johnson, manager of the Aubrey V. Grimes, meat stall at the City Market, continued to feel the pinch caused by food shortages as much as a year after the end of World War II. Grocery ads in the fall of 1946 were heavy with specials on produce and dairy products and an occasional bit of seafood and poultry; but no red meat could be found for sale.

Gene Autry, of Hollywood "singing cowboy" fame, was in Norfolk in the spring of 1948 to speak to the Norfolk Sports Club at Bell's Restaurant. While in Norfolk, he took time to visit a young fan in the hospital.

A favorite way for a young lad to spend a summer afternoon—it's "All Aboard" the tots' train at Ocean View Amusement Park in 1948. One youngster appears to have his eye on the conductor's job.

Norfolk's Battling Palms at their home field, Norfolk Community Field near Booker T. Washington High School, in 1952. The Palms were one of the most popular and longest-running African-American baseball teams in the South, playing ball from the 1920s until 1955.

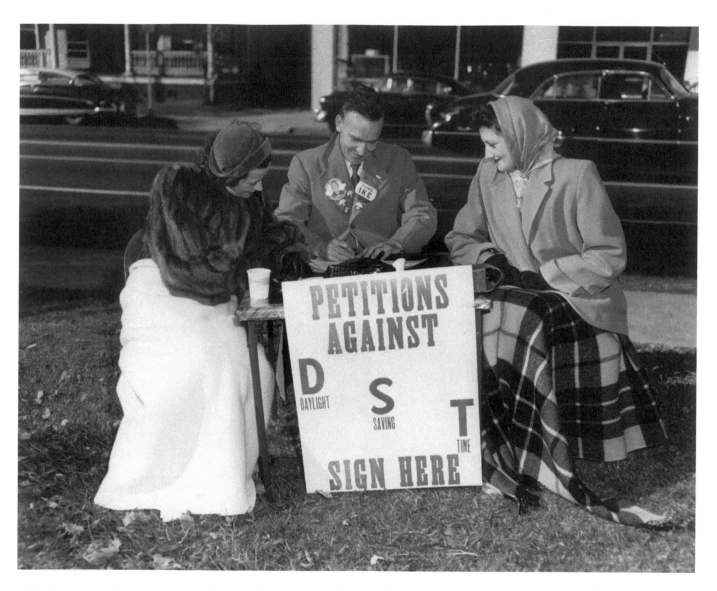

Daylight saving time was introduced to the United States in 1918 and was observed year-round nationwide during World Wars I and II. In other years, it was a local option, often found to be more of a nuisance than a blessing as some communities observed it while their neighbors did not. In a 1952 referendum, Norfolk, Portsmouth, South Norfolk, and Princess Anne County voted to observe. Norfolk county remained on standard time until July, inspiring at least one county resident who worked in the city to wear two wristwatches. In 1953 we elected to stay on standard time by more than 2,400 votes.

Admiral Richard Byrd (1888–1957) led several expeditions to Antarctica between 1928 and 1955. For his second expedition, Byrd procured this long-range, twin-engine Curtiss Wright Condor seaplane, photographed here in 1933, which he named the *William Horlick* after one of the supporters of the expedition. In January 1947, the Norfolk Public Library loaned 12 books to one of Admiral Byrd's expeditions. The admiral took the books to the South Pole and there established a "branch library."

Boarding the streetcar in front of the Granby Street entrance to the Monticello Hotel, 1940s, for the long ride out to Ocean View and Willoughby. Norfolk began to phase out its fleet of streetcars in 1935 in favor of buses, but brought the streetcars back during World War II, when an enormous influx of military and civilian defense workers and their families stretched every amenity—including transportation—to the bursting point.

Australian merchant seaman Elwynn Hepple lost his life on the night of May 16, 1948, when he jumped into the chilly waters of Hampton Roads to rescue two local women from a capsized pleasure boat. Hepple was buried at Forest Lawn Cemetery in a plot provided free of charge by the city of Norfolk. The Civitan Club of Norfolk erected this monument to the seaman on October 30, 1948, and established the Elwynn Hepple Award for Valor, given as appropriate to those whose acts of bravery have far exceeded the norm.

The portion of East Main Street between Commercial Place and Church Street (now St. Paul's Boulevard) was notorious among servicemen all over the world until well after World War II. The few short blocks were packed elbow to elbow with taverns, pawn shops, tattoo parlors, shooting galleries, and burlesque theaters, as seen in this image from 1948.

Locals and enlisted men watch as the Victoria Hotel comes down in the name of redevelopment. The onlookers may be thinking of happy times spent in the hotel's basement restaurant, the Rathskeller, or in the audience at the nearby Gaiety burlesque house.

Main Street at Nebraska Street in May 1959, showing the former Gladstone Hotel. The Union Mission occupied the Gladstone from 1919 until the building was razed during the redevelopment of downtown Norfolk in the early 1960s.

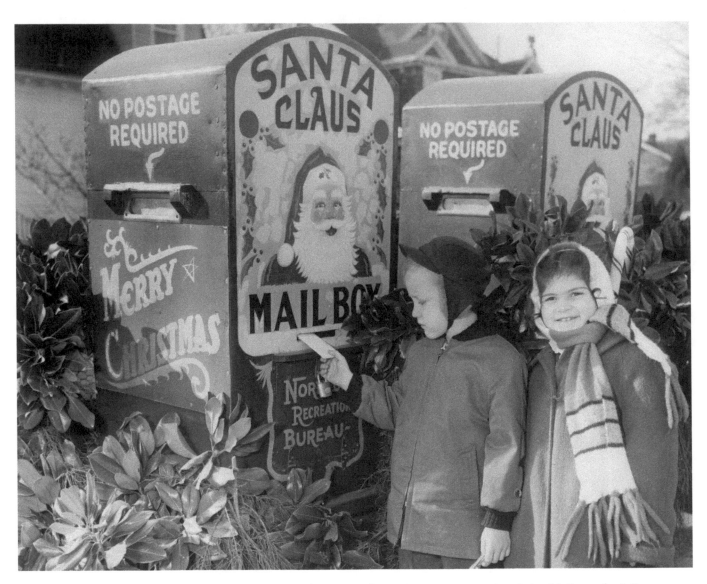

Childhood—when your heart's desire may be just a mailbox away. These youngsters are posting their wish list to the Jolly Old Elf in a special letter box provided by Norfolk's Recreation Bureau. Then it's home to bed to dream of sugar plums and reindeer dancing on the rooftop.

WTAR (now WTKR) was Norfolk's pioneer television broadcasting station when it began to air CBS programming on Channel 4 in 1950. Consumers flocked to the Municipal Arena, where vendors vied to be the one to sell each a first television set.

It's lunchtime for sea lions at the Norfolk Zoo and an expectant crowd gathers as the animals put on a show, with much clapping and barking in anticipation of a nice meal of fresh fish.

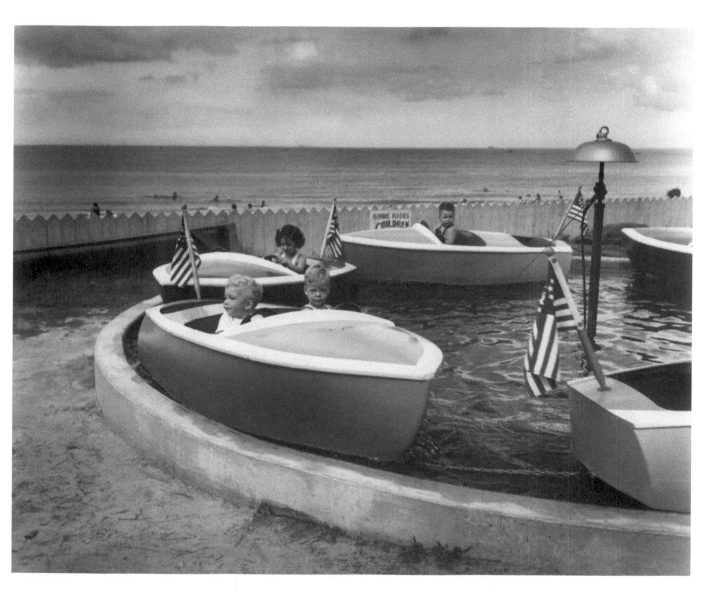

These pint-sized skippers take to the briny in the kiddie boat concession at Ocean View Park, July 1950.

Still active here in 1960, the Union Station on East Main Street served passengers traveling on the Norfolk and Western Railroad from 1912 until the building was demolished in 1963.

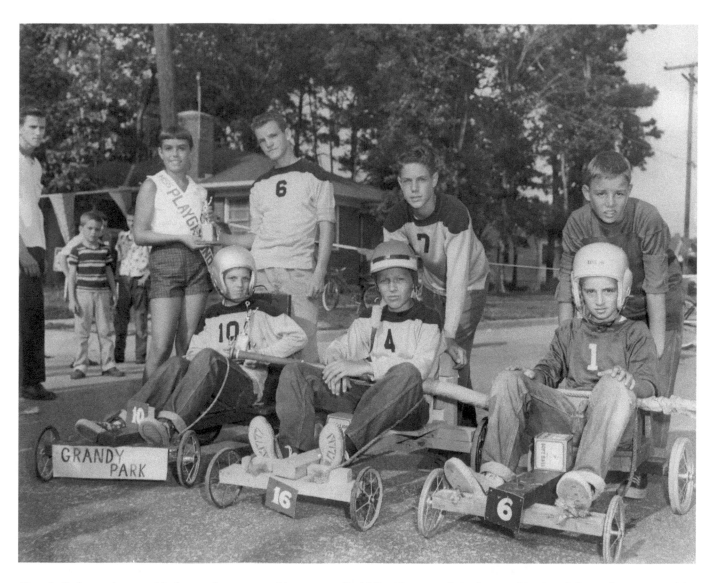

Grandy Park goes home with the trophy, presented by a ponytailed Miss Playground, in the 1956 Pushmobile Derby sponsored by the Norfolk Recreation Bureau. The teams numbered 16 and 6 won the Consolation Prize and the Booby Prize, respectively.

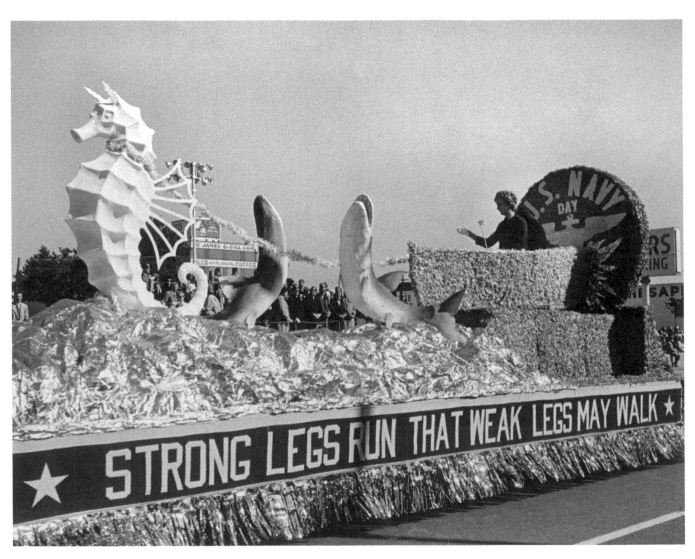

The annual Oyster Bowl football game, sponsored by the local Shriners, raised money for the care and treatment of disabled children under the slogan "Strong Legs Run That Weak Legs May Walk." The parade, with its marching bands, majorettes, floats, clowns, and Shriners weaving in and out on undersized vehicles, was a favorite pregame event, as here in 1963.

A view of the rides at Ocean View Park from the shade of the picnic pavilion. The Ferris wheel can be seen in the near distance. The tower in front of the Ferris wheel supports the Rocket Ship, a descendant of the Circle Swing, which was Ocean View Park's first electric ride, installed in 1906.

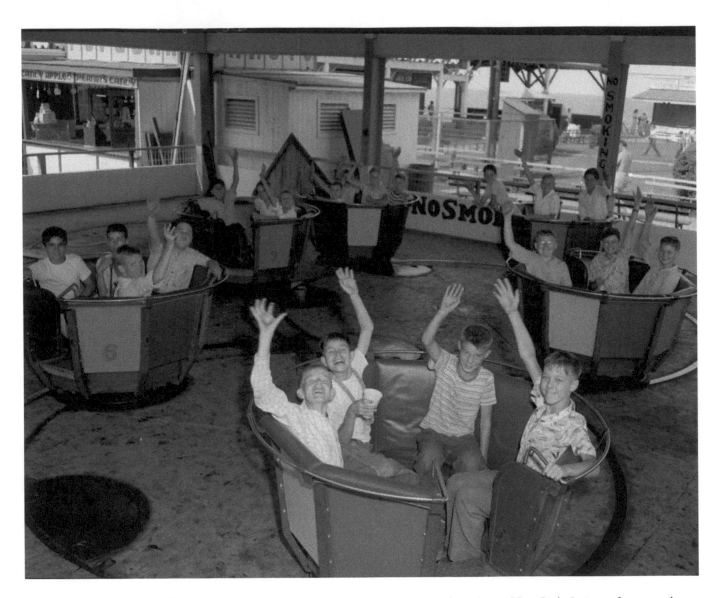

Round and round and round you go, stirring up nothing but fun on the teacup ride at Ocean View Park. In just a few years these young men will probably learn that the teacup ride is also an excellent opportunity to give your best girl a hug as the whirling cup slides her in your direction. All in good fun.

This snapshot, probably taken outside of Arthur's Drug Store on Church Street around 1965, could have been a scene of coming of age anywhere in America. A soda shop, your best girlfriends, a secret to share a laugh over—and a memory to last a lifetime.

Looking east on Main Street near Commerce Street in April 1968. The brand-new Virginia National Bank Building, to the right, towers over its predecessor, the old National Bank of Commerce, directly across the street. At 13 stories, the National Bank of Commerce was Norfolk's tallest building until the late 1950s. The 23-story VNB building left the Bank of Commerce in the dust and remained Norfolk's tallest building into the late 1980s.

Norfolk initiated the International Azalea Festival in 1954 to honor a NATO nation annually in April, when Norfolk is abloom with azaleas. Bonnie Ruth Buchanan, the daughter of U.S. State Department Chief of Protocol Wiley Buchanan, served as Queen Azalea VI. Here she waves from her perch on the back of a Thunderbird convertible during the 1959 festival parade on Granby Street.

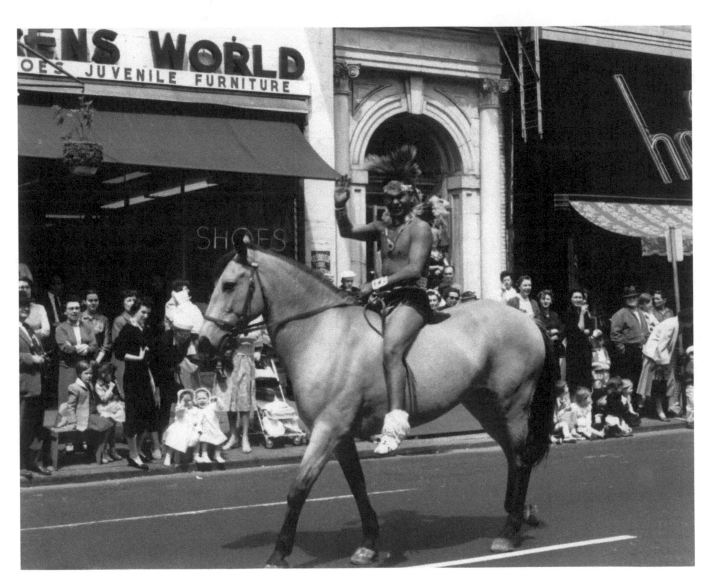

The Azalea Festival Parade, with an American Indian on horseback, progresses down Granby Street, April 6, 1959.

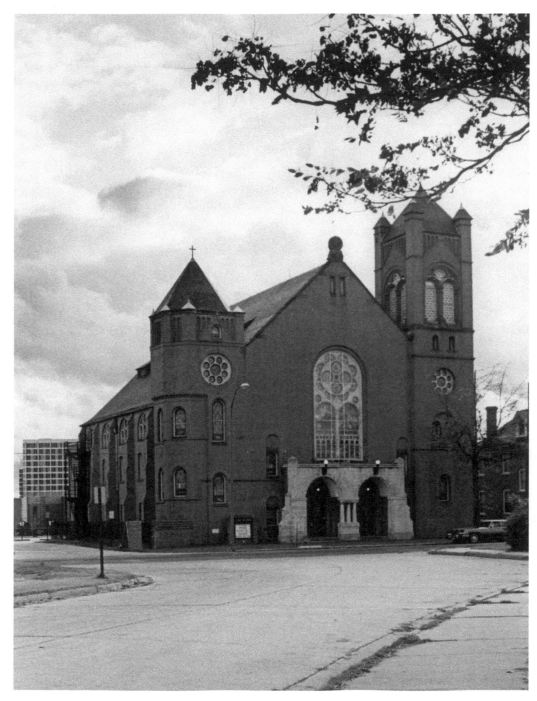

A mission for slaves was begun by the Cumberland Street Methodist Episcopal Church around 1840. The congregation grew, and by 1863 there were more than 800 members. The church became a part of the African Methodist Episcopal Church the same year. The present church was built on Bute Street in 1888 and included the first pipe organ in an African-American church in Virginia.

A view of the 400 block of East Main Street in 1959, shortly before the world-renowned taverns and dance halls met with the wrecker's ball during the city's third phase of redevelopment. The last remaining establishments closed on New Year's Eve 1961. Work started on the city's new office-and-financial district the following year.

Gone but not forgotten. Ocean View's wooden "Leap the Dips," a.k.a. "Rocket," a.k.a. "Southern Belle" roller coaster thrilled and terrified riders with its creaking frame and heart-stopping plunges. After the park closed, the roller coaster had one final hurrah as the star of the 1979 made-for-TV disaster movie *Death of Ocean View Park.* When it came time for the coaster to topple, on June 29, 1979, it refused to budge, withstanding three unsuccessful charges of explosives before being brought down by a bulldozer from local contractor E. T. Gersham.

"Bell bottom trousers, coat of navy blue." Enlisted men assigned to Norfolk's Naval Operating Base, with their distinctive pea jackets, middy blouses, and Dixie Cup hats, were a familiar sight downtown when this trio was snapped passing beneath the Monticello Hotel marquee in 1959.

Looking south on Brewer Street from Market Street in February 1960, as the markets and provenders that grew up as adjuncts to the City Market in the 1930s and 1940s are enjoying their final days. The old City Market and Armory were torn down in 1959, to be replaced by the Rennert Building, or "Maritime Tower." Soon these smaller satellites will be gone as well, as much of the old downtown is cleared to make way for a revitalized commercial area.

Charles Emmanuel "Sweet Daddy" Grace founded his first House of Prayer for All People in Charlotte, North Carolina, in 1926. A church was established in Norfolk in the 1930s and, by the time of Bishop Grace's death in 1960, his flock numbered in the thousands, with red, white, and blue–painted Houses of Prayer in 67 large U.S. cities. The congregation worshiped in the East Freemason Street building shown here from 1955 to 1960. The building, constructed in 1828, originally served the congregation of Christ (Episcopal) Church.

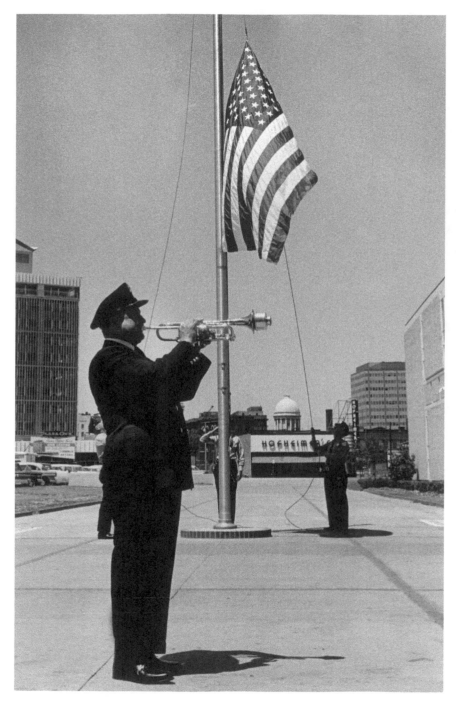

The U.S. Congress enacted National Police Week in October 1962, authorizing President John F. Kennedy to declare May 15 as Peace Officers Memorial Day, when special tribute would be paid annually to fallen officers across the nation. The week in which May 15 falls is observed as Police Memorial Week. Here in May 1963, a Norfolk officer plays "Taps" and the American flag is lowered to half-staff in City Hall plaza in honor and memory of the 28 members of the Norfolk Police Department who had died in the line of duty.

Eastward aerial view on East Main Street from the National Bank of Commerce, around 1962. The City Jail and General District Court building, at upper-left, have just been completed, and ground has been cleared for the rest of the new Civic Center complex—the 2-story Norfolk Circuit Court building and 11-story City Hall.

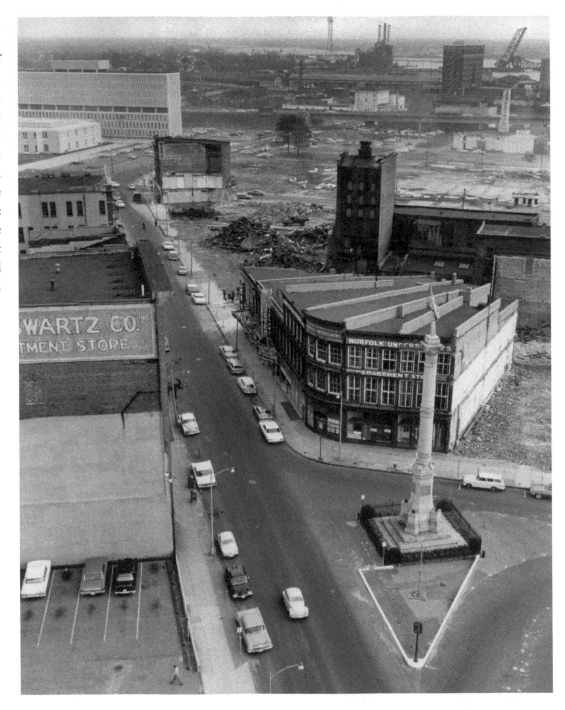

Notes on the Photographs

These notes, listed by page number, attempt to include all aspects known of the photographs. Each of the photographs is identified by the page number, a title or description, photographer and collection, archive, and call or box number when applicable. Although every attempt was made to collect all data, in some cases complete data may have been unavailable due to the age and condition of some of the photographs and records.

Printed in the USA
CPSIA information can be obtained
at www.ICGtesting.com
JSHW072025140824
68134JS00042B/3788